T0055401

PLAYBACK+

Speed • Pitch • Balance • Loop

To access audio visit:
www.halleonard.com/mylibrary

Enter Code
5881-9403-2641-8754

ISBN 978-0-634-09294-7

HAL•LEONARD®
CORPORATION
7777 W. BLUEMOUND RD. P.O. BOX 13819 MILWAUKEE, WI 53213

Al Lerner, composer, arranger, conductor, has been writing and performing for over five decades. His playing includes performances in every major concert hall in the world. He has entertained audiences at Carnegie Hall and even conducted a Royal Command Performance for Queen Elizabeth of England. As a composer, he is the author of over 200 songs, among them, the closing theme, "So Until I See You," for "The Tonight Show with Jack Paar." Motion picture work is yet another aspect of his career. On piano, Al has accompanied some of the greatest artists; his career spans playing with Harry James, Charlie Barnet, and Tommy Dorsey during the wonderful era of the big bands. Dick Haymes, Frankie Laine, Rosemary Clooney, Pat Boone, Jimmie Rodgers and Vic Damone are just a few of the entertainers for

CONTENTS

ALWAYS

Words and Music by
IRVING BERLIN

Moderately slow

APRIL IN PARIS

Music by VERNON DUKE
Words by E.Y. HARBURG

Moderately

Freely

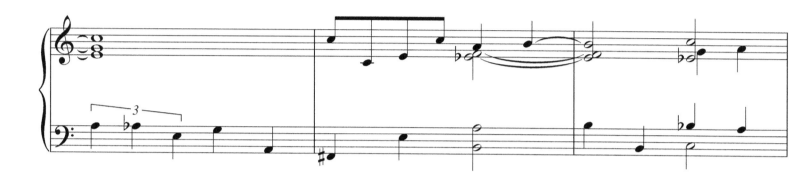

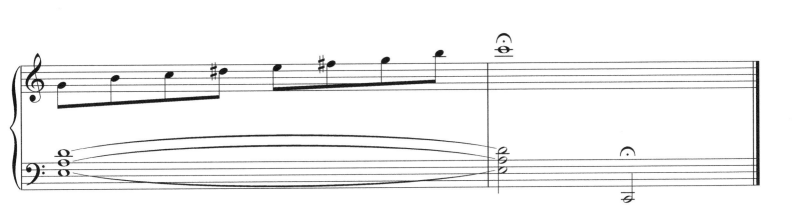

EASY TO LOVE
(You'd Be So Easy to Love)

Words and Music by
COLE PORTER

Moderately

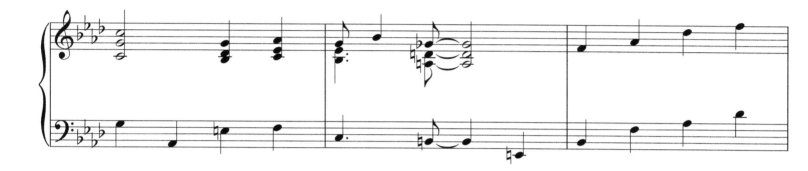

I'M OLD FASHIONED

Words by JOHNNY MERCER
Music by JEROME KERN

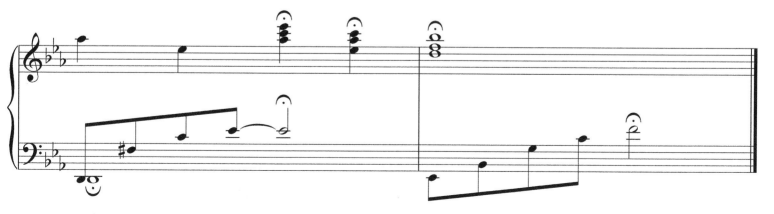

MISTY

Music by ERROLL GARNER

Moderately slow, freely

mf

Easy lilt

rall.

MOON RIVER

from the Paramount Picture BREAKFAST AT TIFFANY'S

Words by JOHNNY MERCER
Music by HENRY MANCINI

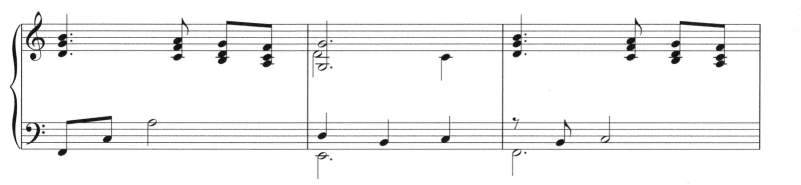

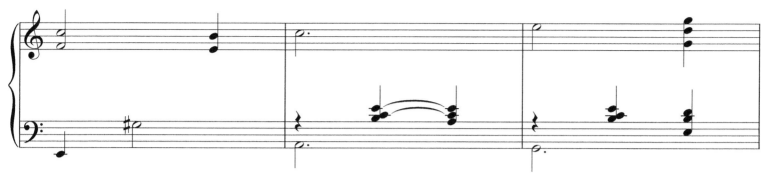

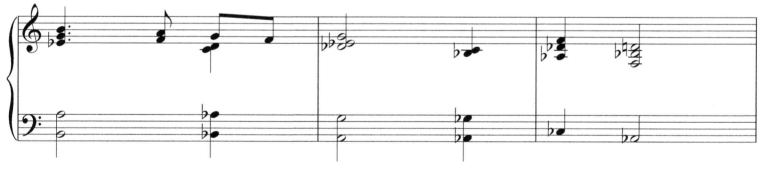

MOONLIGHT BECOMES YOU

from the Paramount Picture ROAD TO MOROCCO

Words by JOHNNY BURKE
Music by JAMES VAN HEUSEN

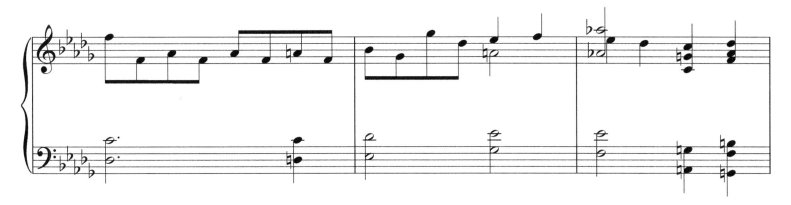

accel.

rall.

OUT OF NOWHERE
from the Paramount Picture DUDE RANCH

Words by EDWARD HEYMAN
Music by JOHNNY GREEN

PEOPLE

Words by BOB MERRILL
Music by JULE STYNE

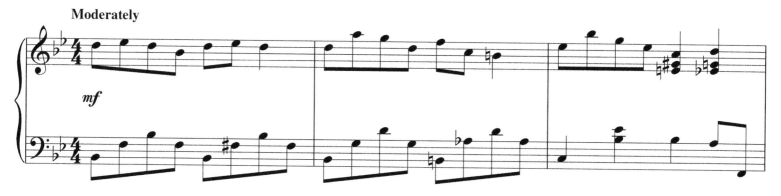

THE SWEETEST SOUNDS

from NO STRINGS

Lyrics and Music by
RICHARD RODGERS

Moderately

TENDERLY

Lyric by JACK LAWRENCE
Music by WALTER GROSS

THERE WILL NEVER BE ANOTHER YOU

Lyric by MACK GORDON
Music by HARRY WARREN

Moderately

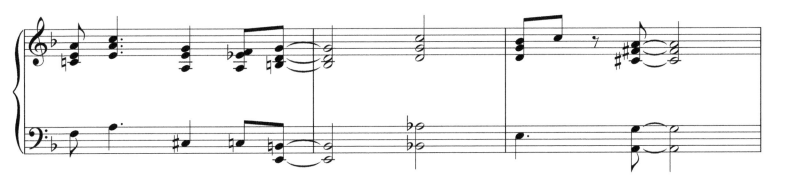

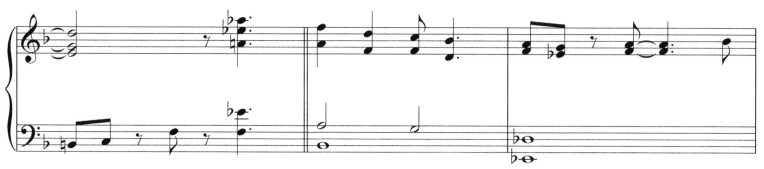

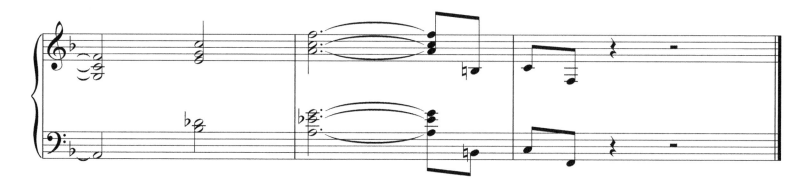

THE WAY YOU LOOK TONIGHT

Words by DOROTHY FIELDS
Music by JEROME KERN

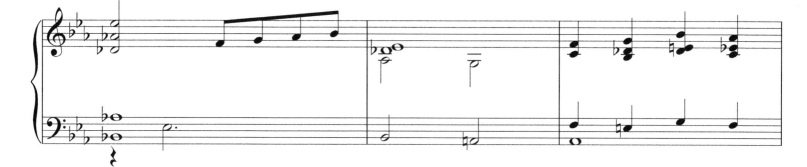

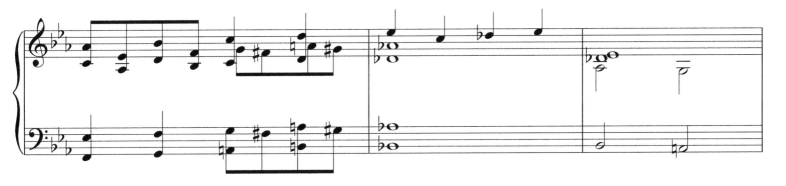

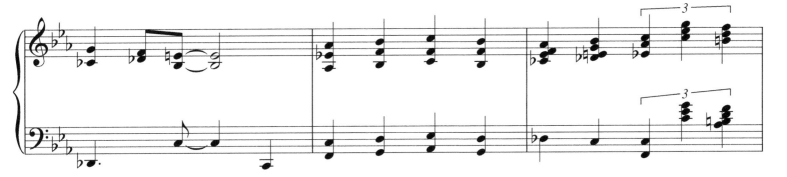

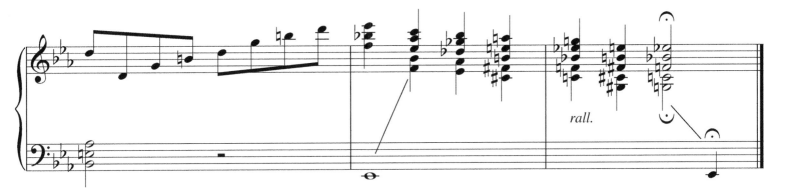

WHEN SUNNY GETS BLUE

Lyric by JACK SEGAL
Music by MARVIN FISHER

Light Blues feel

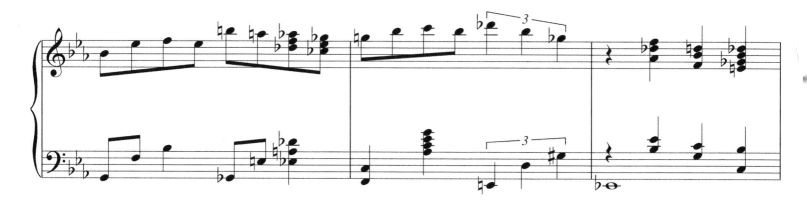

YESTERDAYS

Words by OTTO HARBACH
Music by JEROME KERN

Pensively

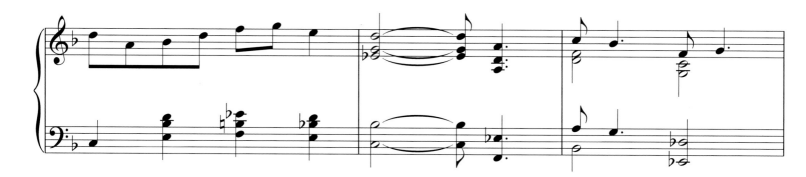

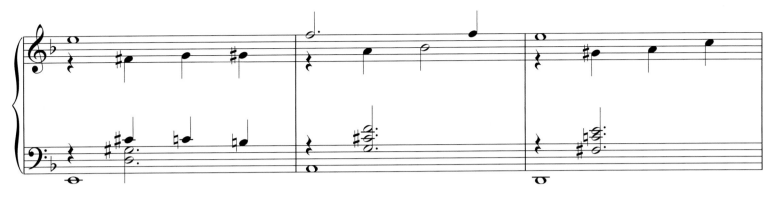

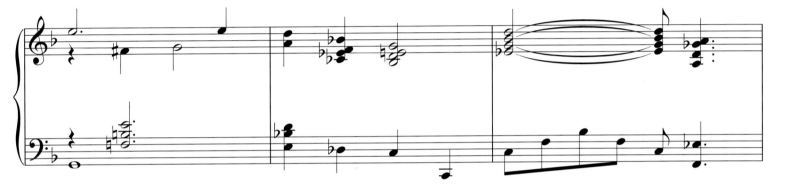

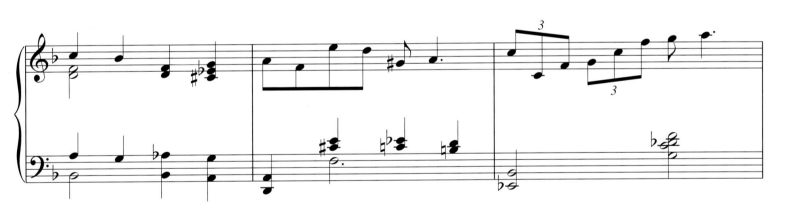

ALL JAZZED UP!

FROM HAL LEONARD

In this series, popular favorites receive unexpected fresh treatments. Uniquely reimagined and crafted for intermediate piano solo, these tunes have been All Jazzed Up!

J.S. BACH
Air on the G String • Aria • Bist du bei mir (Be Thou with Me) • Gavotte • Jesu, Joy of Man's Desiring • Largo • March • Minuet in G • Musette • Sheep May Safely Graze • Siciliano • Sleepers, Awake (Wachet Auf).
00151064...$12.99

THE BEATLES
All My Loving • And I Love Her • Come Together • Eight Days a Week • Eleanor Rigby • The Fool on the Hill • Here, There and Everywhere • Lady Madonna • Lucy in the Sky with Diamonds • Michelle • While My Guitar Gently Weeps • Yesterday.
00172235...$12.99

CHRISTMAS CAROLS
Auld Lang Syne • Deck the Hall • The First Noel • Good King Wenceslas • In the Bleak Midwinter • Jingle Bells • Joy to the World • O Christmas Tree • O Come, All Ye Faithful • O Little Town of Bethlehem • Up on the Housetop • We Wish You a Merry Christmas.
00277866...$12.99

CHRISTMAS SONGS
Blue Christmas • The Christmas Song (Chestnuts Roasting on an Open Fire) • Christmas Time Is Here • Do You Hear What I Hear • Feliz Navidad • Have Yourself a Merry Little Christmas • I'll Be Home for Christmas • Merry Christmas, Darling • Silver Bells • Sleigh Ride • White Christmas • Winter Wonderland.
00236706...$12.99

COLDPLAY
Clocks • Don't Panic • Every Teardrop Is a Waterfall • Fix You • Magic • Paradise • The Scientist • A Sky Full of Stars • Speed of Sound • Trouble • Viva La Vida • Yellow.
00149026...$12.99

DISNEY
Belle • Circle of Life • Cruella De Vil • Ev'rybody Wants to Be a Cat • It's a Small World • Let It Go • Mickey Mouse March • Once upon a Dream • Part of Your World • Supercalifragilisticexpialidocious • Under the Sea • When She Loved Me.
00151072...$14.99

JIMI HENDRIX
Castles Made of Sand • Crosstown Traffic • Fire • Foxey Lady • Hey Joe • Little Wing • Manic Depression • Purple Haze • Spanish Castle Magic • The Wind Cries Mary.
00174441...$12.99

BILLY JOEL
And So It Goes • Honesty • It's Still Rock and Roll to Me • Just the Way You Are • The Longest Time • Lullabye (Goodnight, My Angel) • My Life • New York State of Mind • Piano Man • The River of Dreams • She's Always a Woman • She's Got a Way.
00149039...$12.99

MOTOWN
Ain't Nothing like the Real Thing • How Sweet It Is (To Be Loved by You) • I Can't Help Myself (Sugar Pie, Honey Bunch) • I Heard It Through the Grapevine • I Want You Back • Let's Get It On • My Girl • Never Can Say Goodbye • Overjoyed • Papa Was a Rollin' Stone • Still • You Can't Hurry Love.
00174482...$12.99

NIRVANA
About a Girl • All Apologies • Come as You Are • Dumb • Heart Shaped Box • In Bloom • Lithium • The Man Who Sold the World • On a Plain • (New Wave) Polly • Rape Me • Smells like Teen Spirit.
00149025...$12.99

OZZY OSBOURNE
Crazy Train • Dreamer • Flying High Again • Goodbye to Romance • Iron Man • Mama, I'm Coming Home • Mr. Crowley • No More Tears • Over the Mountain • Paranoid • Perry Mason • Time After Time.
00149040...$12.99

ELVIS PRESLEY
Blue Suede Shoes • Can't Help Falling in Love • Cryin' in the Chapel • Don't • Don't Be Cruel (To a Heart That's True) • Heartbreak Hotel • I Want You, I Need You, I Love You • Jailhouse Rock • Love Me Tender • Suspicious Minds • The Wonder of You • You Don't Have to Say You Love Me.
00198895...$12.99

STEVIE WONDER
As • Ebony and Ivory • For Once in My Life • I Just Called to Say I Love You • I Wish • Isn't She Lovely • My Cherie Amour • Ribbon in the Sky • Signed, Sealed, Delivered I'm Yours • Sir Duke • Superstition • You Are the Sunshine of My Life.
00149090...$12.99

HAL•LEONARD®
www.halleonard.com

Prices, contents and availability subject to change without notice.

Disney characters and artwork © Disney Enterprises, Inc.

0618